GO
MOBILIZE

INVITING OTHERS TO JOIN YOU IN
LIVING OUT GOD'S GLOBAL PURPOSE

Go Mobilize
Copyright © 2013-2022 by Center for Mission Mobilization
All rights reserved. No part of this publication may be reproduced in
any form without written permission from the publisher.

ISBN: 978-0-9825107-8-0

Published by Center for Mission Mobilization
PO Box 3556
Fayetteville, AR 72702
For more resources, visit mobilization.org/resources

Translations
We desire to make this material available to as many as will use it around the world
in a way that honors everyone involved in the work. If you would like to translate or
adapt this resource to use in your cultural context, we are very open to collaborating
with you. There are guidelines for translators at mobilization.org/translation.

Printed in the United States of America.

First Edition, Eighth Imprint, 2022.
C: 06-13-14   M: 01-26-22 11:01 AM

CONTENTS

INTRODUCTION

Beliefs and convictions. They might seem like the same thing, but there is a big difference between the two. I believe in the importance of family, so I try to put the needs of my family ahead of my own.

Their happiness comes before mine. This belief is important to me, and I try my best to make sure I live it out on a daily basis.

I also believe in democracy, but I don't always vote in my country's elections. I believe in not judging others, yet I'm frequently guilty of making assumptions and judging people based on those assumptions.

Why do some of my beliefs affect the way I live my life, while others don't? The answer is the difference between beliefs and convictions.

Someone once said, "a belief is something that you hold. A conviction is something that holds you." We all hold lots of beliefs, but few of our beliefs become convictions. Beliefs are things we give mental assent to. We tend to think of the mind when we talk about beliefs.

Beliefs become convictions when they direct the way we live our lives. When we talk about convictions we use words like passion, burden, and dedication. We tend to think of the heart and the hands when we talk about convictions.

So what does this have to do with *Go Mobilize*? Simply put, *Go Mobilize* is a study about convictions.

Almost any Christian would say they believe in the Great Commission. You could even ask them if they believe God desires every believer to be involved in seeing the Great Commission fulfilled and they will likely tell you they do.

So why then do so few Christians (and churches, for that matter) actively participate in taking the gospel to the least reached? Why is it that the harvest is still so great and the laborers are still so few?

Go Mobilize is a study about turning beliefs into convictions. It's really about gaining one big conviction: that God has called all believers to join Him in reaching the nations with the gospel. Along with that are several supporting convictions: 1) a relational approach to mobilization is best, 2) priority should be placed on reaching the unreached, and 3) we must model the lifestyle we are inviting others to join.

Throughout the 7 lessons of *Go Mobilize*, we will show how you can invite others to move beyond simply believing in the Great Commission to being convicted about it. To that end, a significant question every follower of Jesus and every church must answer is, "What part of your life reflects God's heart for all peoples?" Do we simply believe the Great Commission, or are we convicted about it in such way that it changes our lives? *Go Mobilize* equips you to practically live a lifestyle of inviting others to join you in living out God's global purpose.

USING GO MOBILIZE
You can use this book in a small group, as a Sunday school class, with a group of friends, or even in a one-on-one relationship. If nothing else, read it yourself and then find someone to go through it with you. Community and partnership are essential in the Kingdom of God!

Each lesson involves an article, a Go Discuss, Go To The Word, Go Mobilize, and Go Pray section.

The *Go Mobilize* study is designed as a follow-up to the *Xplore* study, but can be used by any Christians who are excited about and living out God's heart for the world. You can order hard copies or free digital copies of *Xplore* and *Go Mobilize* at mobilization.org.

With this said, let's *Go Mobilize!*

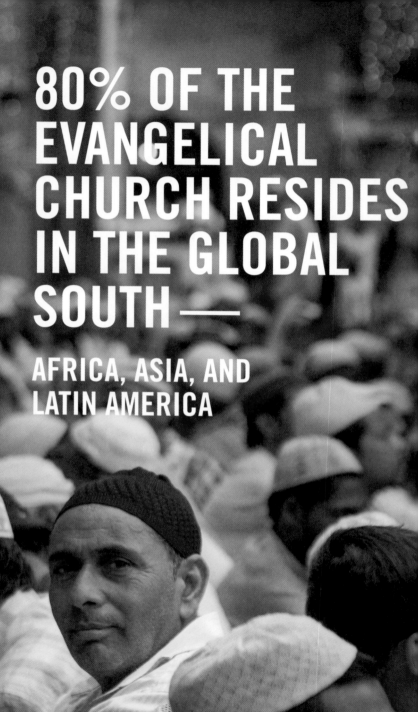

80% OF THE EVANGELICAL CHURCH RESIDES IN THE GLOBAL SOUTH—

AFRICA, ASIA, AND LATIN AMERICA

LESSON 1
WHAT IS MOBILIZATION?

"WE MUST BE GLOBAL CHRISTIANS WITH A GLOBAL VISION BECAUSE OUR GOD IS A GLOBAL GOD." — JOHN STOTT

To mobilize is to awaken, excite, inspire, provoke, stimulate, galvanize, and encourage groups of people toward some specific action. In the English language, the word "mobilize" is traditionally a military term. It refers to the process of moving resources, soldiers, weapons, and supplies toward the battlefield. Without wartime mobilization, soldiers would never make it to the battlefield. Battles could not be fought. Wars could not be won.

Mobilization is critical to the act of making war. In most armies, for every soldier who fights on the front lines, about 10 more personnel are needed to support that one soldier with supplies, tactics, technology, communication, and medical care. Mobilization is about much more than getting the soldiers to the front line, fully equipped with everything they need to execute the battle plan. It involves thousands of people laboring behind the scenes, who are offering support and resources to the soldiers.

MOBILIZATION TO MISSION

The Body of Christ wages a different kind of war. Mission mobilization, simply put, is pointing people who know Jesus to entire peoples who don't. The goal of mission mobilization is to help Christians worldwide see that Jesus' commission to go and make disciples of all nations is for each of us. As mobilizers, we want to open believers' eyes to the breadth of ways to be involved in Great Commission work, in addition to being a "soldier," or full-time ministry worker.

When we discuss mobilization, our focus is on helping believers prioritize mission to the unreached. Mobilizing God's people to get involved in any Christian activity is good. However, since Jesus placed an emphasis on making disciples among all nations, shouldn't our mobilization have the same emphasis? Doesn't it, therefore, make sense to focus our mobilization efforts on increasing attention, resources, and passion toward the unreached?

And how exactly should we go about doing this? As mobilizers, we seek to influence people through relationships. We invite others to join us strategically, as we engage them relationally. Jesus was a master at this. He had a great vision, but spent three years intentionally discipling a few men. The method of the master wasn't a program. The method of the master was to build up people. While we may use programs in our ministry, the program's most effective use is in how it helps facilitate relationships and spiritual formation.

The ultimate job of a mission mobilizer is to engage, equip, and connect believers — and churches — worldwide to their most strategic role in fulfilling the Great Commission. But where do we begin?

Nearly all the tools, methods, and approaches to mobilization can be boiled down to three stages of development: show believers the Word of God; show believers the world God loves; and show believers the work God has called them to. By focusing on these three areas, God's Word, God's world, and God's work, a mobilizer can help individual Christians connect with the Great Commission in ways they are passionate about.

THE THREE STEPS TO MOBILIZING OTHERS

1. God's Word—The first step in development is showing others the biblical basis of missions in God's Word. The goal is to demonstrate that, all along, from Genesis to Revelation, God has had a plan to reach all nations. And that plan involves His people working in coordination with Him and His will.

This is exactly what Jesus did after His resurrection when He appeared to His disciples. Luke 24:45-47 says, "Then He opened their minds so they could understand the Scriptures. He told them, 'This is what is written: The Messiah will suffer and rise from the dead on the third day, and repentance for the forgiveness of sins will be preached in His name to all nations, beginning at Jerusalem.'"

Jesus used the Scriptures, in this case the Old Testament, to show His followers that the message of His death, resurrection, and provision of salvation is now available to all and must be preached to all nations. In this passage, Jesus is modeling for us the need to help Christians understand from Scripture the global implications of His salvation.

In Lesson 4, we will go into greater detail about the importance of establishing a biblical basis of missions.

2. God's World—The second step of development in mission mobilization is helping Christians understand God's world. William Carey once said, "To know the will of God, we need an open Bible and an open map." There are more than 7 billion people in the world today from thousands of different cultures, languages, and beliefs. Helping believers to understand God's world is to help them come to grips with the current realities on earth and determine the most strategic steps to reach the lost.

For nearly 2,000 years, courageous men and women of faith have taken up the call to spread the message of Jesus to the ends of the earth. And in many areas, the church has been successful in spreading the gospel. But there are still large pockets of the world where there is no Christian witness.

Once again, we must look to Jesus as our model for effective mobilization. Jesus said in Matthew 9:37-38, "The harvest is plentiful, but the laborers are few; therefore pray earnestly to the Lord of the harvest to send out laborers into His harvest" (see also Luke 10:2). Jesus mobilized the disciples into action by demonstrating the great imbalance between the harvest and the needed laborers. If the gospel is to be taken to the nations, more laborers are needed.

Believers need to understand the reality of God's world. Put another way, we must understand the current situation in the world as it relates to world evangelization.

If the gospel is to be preached to all nations, where does it still need to go? One effective and memorable way to show a Christian the world's situation is with the THUMB acrostic. In Lesson 5, we will go into more detail about this tool and how it can be used.

3. God's Work—The third step in mobilization is showing believers what it looks like to participate in God's work to reach the nations. This is a crucial step in the mobilization process. Mobilizers can inspire Christians with the Word of God and challenge them with reaching the unreached, but if they cannot connect others to this vision practically, they have failed.

The Bible clearly calls all believers to use their talents and resources to further His mission. All are called. But how each believer lives this teaching depends upon his or her skills, talents, gifts, and abilities. That is why we focus on what is referred to as the World Christian lifestyle.

What is a World Christian? World Christians are followers of Jesus Christ that understand, from Scripture, God's heart for the world and His invitation for each believer to participate in His global purpose. They understand the current state of the world and the billions that are unreached with hope in Jesus. And they have chosen to let these beliefs develop into a conviction leading to participation in the completion of the Great Commission. They have chosen to join God in His work by centering their lives around the goal of seeing Jesus glorified among all peoples.

In Lesson 6, we focus on five main habits Christians can adopt in order to live the World Christian lifestyle: praying, going, sending, welcoming and mobilizing. In this crucial third step, you will learn how you can encourage Christians to participate in fulfilling the Great Commission in specific and strategic ways.

We believe mobilization can be part of everyone's lifestyle, no matter your personality type, gifting, or skill set. As you learn about and live out these three steps of mobilization, you will naturally mobilize people toward the nations. Look for ways to integrate this approach into your lifestyle. The point is not how many believers you can influence at one given time, but rather a sustained influence over a long period of time.

GO ▶ DISCUSS

Consider Jesus' words, "The harvest is plentiful but the laborers are few…" (Luke 10:2). Why do you think more Christians aren't burdened with sending laborers to the unreached?

_____
_____
_____

How would you verbalize your own burden that laborers be raised up and sent to the unreached?

_____
_____
_____

In your own words, why do you believe mobilization is crucial in the church?

_____
_____
_____

How would a strategy of raising up mobilizers result in more cross-cultural goers to the unreached?

_____
_____
_____
_____

GO ▶ TO THE WORD

Read 1 Corinthians 3:6-9.
Describe the different roles present in this passage. What does man do? What does God do?

_____

_____

_____

_____

_____

Read Romans 10:13-15.
Describe the progression outlined in the text. Who is involved? How does it all begin?

_____

_____

_____

_____

_____

Who was mobilized in this passage and what were they mobilized to do?

_____

_____

_____

_____

GO ▶ MOBILIZE

Find one or two people who are passionate about mission in your church or community. Spend some time with them and ask how they gained a heart for mission and how they stay connected to God's heart for the whole world.

Before the next meeting, read the boxed portion of Mobilization Works on page 41. Also, review the material in Lesson 1, paying specific attention to the three steps of development: God's Word, God's world, and God's work. In your own words, describe what you think a World Christian is. Bring to the next meeting your thoughts on multiplication and how you would describe a World Christian. Share these thoughts with the group.

GO ▶ PRAY

Following the example of Matthew 9:37-38, pray that laborers would be raised up and sent out. Specifically, pray that God would raise up a new movement of goers from among the millions of evangelicals that have strategic access to the unreached—countries such as Brazil, China, India, Indonesia, and Nigeria.

Pray that God would teach you how to make mobilization a part of your personal ministry strategy.

Pray that God would spark a mission movement in your church, ministry, campus, or town, and that He would raise up mission mobilizers.

TOTAL EVANGELICALS WORLDWIDE: 546 MILLION

LESSON 2
QUALITIES OF AN EFFECTIVE MOBILIZER

> "I CAME TO YOU IN WEAKNESS WITH GREAT FEAR AND TREMBLING. MY MESSAGE AND MY PREACHING WERE NOT WITH WISE AND PERSUASIVE WORDS, BUT WITH A DEMONSTRATION OF THE SPIRIT'S POWER, SO THAT YOUR FAITH MIGHT NOT REST ON HUMAN WISDOM, BUT ON GOD'S POWER."
> —1 CORINTHIANS 2:3-5

A mobilizer often struggles with an internal conflict between going to the field and staying to mobilize others. Todd Ahrend, the international director of The Traveling Team (a mobilization ministry), and his wife once had to ask themselves this tough question: "Do we want to be the missionaries, or do we want to multiply the missionaries?" They had to make a decision whether to be the goers who would labor for God to reach the unreached or whether they would focus on mobilizing others toward the unreached.

The difficulty lies in the fact that mobilizers, just like other World Christians, are passionate about the lost. They have a fire in them to see Christ and His gospel taken to the farthest ends of the earth. They have made it their life's purpose to see the fulfillment of the Great Commission. They want to be on the front lines, sharing the gospel and planting new churches. They long to share life with people who have very few opportunities to meet Christ followers.

But they stay—not because of fear, finances, or the challenges of crossing cultures. Mobilizers stay because deep down they are convinced that the most strategic role they can play is to rally the church toward a greater involvement in completing the Great Commission. They strive to raise both awareness and passion for

frontier mission among churches and Christian fellowships. Mobilizers educate, promote, and connect believers to their most strategic roles. Not every Christian is called to go to another place and personally reach the unreached, but all Christians are called to participate in seeing them reached!

But to be a good mobilizer, it takes more than passion for frontier mission and knowledge of the world. Many passionate and well inten-tioned mobilizers have turned others away from cross-cultural ministry through aggressive and overly zealous tactics. I remember feeling insult-ed the first time I heard about the thousands of unreached people groups, the 10/40 Window, and the persecuted church. It wasn't that I didn't agree biblically with what I heard or see the importance of taking the gospel to those who had yet to hear. What I objected to was how they made me feel about myself as a Christian. Suddenly, because I was not going to work in the 10/40 Window, all the ministry I had done, all the worship I had given God, all my plans to live a life dedicated to the Lord felt as though it was not good enough. In some ways, guilt tactics made me feel like a second-class citizen.

At one time or another, many of us have felt guilty as we listened to a mission talk about how broken and lost the world is. But as mobilizers, we have the privilege of taking fellow Christians on a wonderful journey. We get to be their tour guide as we travel throughout the world, introducing them to the tens of thousands of diverse people groups that God loves. We are their teachers as we walk them through Scripture, weaving together the global thread of God's heart for all peoples throughout the Bible. We get to be the ones to tell them exciting stories of entire cultures being transformed by Jesus Christ.

WHAT DOES IT TAKE TO BE AN EFFECTIVE MOBILIZER?

We have put together a short list of qualities we believe to be crucial for effective mobilization. Note that none of these are personality traits or talents, but rather attitudes and habits. None of us has to be perfect in all these qualities, but through the power of the Holy Spirit, we each have the capacity to adopt these qualities and continue growing in them.

Be a Servant—Why would any church want to listen to someone who is not first a servant and second a mobilizer? Are you serving people in your local church? Are you actively involved in advancing the vision of your local church? Are you actively being a blessing to your church in heart and action? Are you giving to your local church? It can be easy to sit back and judge, but a true mobilizer is a servant.

Be a Well-Rounded Person—Be someone people can relate to. Have other interests and passions in addition to mission. Have hobbies. Take vacations. Have a favorite sports team. Don't steer every conversation toward mission. You never know when God is going to use one of your interests, talents, or passions as a vehicle for mobilization.

Know the Word of God—Do you know God's Word? Can you teach from it? On topics other than mission? A mobilizer should be a student of the Word and able to teach from the Scripture on many topics, not just those

that are mission-related. This is another part of being a well-rounded person.

Pray—We must be men and women who are connected to our Father in heaven, listening to Him, talking to Him, fellowshipping with Him. Through prayer we are changed by God, and through prayer we join Him in changing circumstances around us. As we pray, we will intercede for many people, including goers, the unreached, and the churches on the front lines of God's mission.

Value Other Ministries (Have a Kingdom Mindset)—Value the various types of ministries you encounter and encourage those who are active in ministry. Don't look down upon a person because their ministry does not have a global reach. Rather, encourage them and be grateful to God for the work they do. Find common ground. Work together to see how mobilization might be made a part of their ministry.

Be an Evangelist—Be on the lookout for opportunities to share Christ with those around you. Just because your neighbor is not a member of unreached Fulakunda of Senegal does not take away your responsibility to be a witness of Jesus Christ to them.

Value People and Principles—Always put people over programs and prioritize principles over tools. Mobilization is about people, not programs. It's about pointing people who know and follow Jesus to entire peoples that don't. We value seeing God's people striving to make disciples of all nations. We should never let our methodologies interfere with the task of mobilization, nor do we exalt a man-made tool over biblical principles.

Be a Learner—Mobilizers should be permanent students, always looking to increase their knowledge base. Here are a few examples of areas we think are worth investing in: current world events, the major religions of the world, theology, general Bible knowledge, foreign languages, and current church trends.

Be an Optimist—Mobilizers spend a lot of time hearing why people are not or cannot be involved in completing the Great Commission. It can be discouraging to listen to so many excuses, but optimism is contagious. Mobilizers need be the type of Christians who, like William Carey, believe that we should "Expect great things from God. Attempt great things for God." An optimistic mobilizer can model, and pass on to others the belief and confidence that God can and will use us to change the world. Through prayer and study of Scripture, we can cultivate a godly optimism.

GO ▶ DISCUSS

In which of these qualities do you think you are strongest? Weakest? What are some practical ways you would like to grow in any of these qualities?

Can you think of any qualities or characteristics of good mobilizers that were not listed above?

Who do you know that exemplifies one or more of these qualities?

What are some negative repercussions that may arise for a mobilizer without these qualities?

GO ▶ TO THE WORD

Read 1 Corinthians 2.

In 1 Corinthians 2, Paul mentions six times that Christians should "speak" or communicate God's truth (see verses 1-7, 12-13). What are the types of speech that Paul is trying to avoid? What is he trying to model?

_____

_____

_____

Based on this passage, what are some of Paul's qualities that we as mobilizers should adopt to better communicate God's plan to reach all nations?

_____

_____

_____

GO ▶ MOBILIZE

Based on your group discussion, what are the areas in which you want to begin growing? Are there actions you can take this week to grow in these areas? Write down your application in the space below, along with today's date.

_____

_____

_____

Make an appointment to talk with one of your pastors this week. Tell them you want to know more about the vision and mission of your church. Find out if your church has a mission statement and familiarize yourself with the key tenets. Pray regularly for the vision of your church and what role you have to play in accomplishing it.

GO ▶ PRAY

Pray that God would show you how you can become a better mobilizer. Be sure to spend some time praying that God would help you speak the wisdom of God as you mobilize others.

2.9 BILLION PEOPLE ARE STILL UNREACHED WITH THE GOSPEL

LESSON 3
THE URGENCY OF MOBILIZATION

"INDEED, THE RIGHT TIME IS NOW. TODAY IS THE DAY OF SALVATION."
—2 CORINTHIANS 6:2B

In August 2010, there was a massive cave-in at the Copiapó mining facility deep in the heart of the Atacama Desert in Chile. Seventeen days later, to the surprise of rescue personnel, a note was discovered taped to the end of a drill bit after it had penetrated an area they thought might contain the trapped miners. The note simply read, "Estamos bien en el refugio, los 33," or, "We are all well in the shelter, the 33 of us!" Many people would describe what happened next as a miracle.

Countries rallied together to organize a rescue effort within just a few short days. Three large multinational drilling teams and their equipment were airlifted to the remote Chilean desert. Each team drilled an escape tunnel in an attempt to reach and rescue the 33 miners trapped more than 2,300 feet under ground. While the rescue tunnels were being drilled, the Chilean Navy, along with help from the U.S. space agency, NASA, were developing three state-of-the art rescue capsules named Fénix 1, 2, and 3. Nearly every Chilean government agency and dozens of other corporations from almost every continent were also on hand to help with rescue efforts.

After being trapped for more than 69 days, setting a record for the longest time spent under ground, all 33 miners were rescued and brought to the surface in the three Fénix rescue pods. Approximately 1 billion people watched the rescue live on television and the total cost of the global rescue initiative was more than $20 million (USD).

By contrast, we live in a world of instant news where websites, Facebook, Twitter, and 24-hour news channels bombard us with urgent, critical, and desperate appeals, but move us to little meaningful action. Some of these appeals are for legitimate and worthy causes. But more often we are bombarded with the mundane, to the point we miss the deserving. Many of these urgent appeals ask us to simply "like" a cause, "share" a post, "re-tweet," or change our profile picture to show our support. We are led to believe that if a Facebook post is "liked" a certain amount of times or if enough people change their status messages, then a child will receive a life-saving operation or money will be given to feed starving children. Simply put, it is easy for Christians today to feel as though they are living a life of significance, supporting organizations and helping to change the world, but with little to no personal investment or sacrifice.

What is missing from many of our local churches is the type of urgency that produced the rescue efforts that saved the Chilean miners. As the body of Christ, we need to possess a commitment to see every tribe, tongue, and nation bringing glory to God, as well as an awareness of what must be done to complete that task. Mobilization is the critical link connecting the body of Christ with her God-given mission.

And a sense of the acute global need helps us to transition believers from being spectators of the Great Commission to being active and committed participants.

There are three things that mobilizers can do to help instill a critical desire to see Christ preached among all nations:

1. Demonstrate the Word as the Source of Our Urgency—The Scriptures abound with passages that communicate an urgency to complete the Great Commission. Reading the Word of God should remind us of the task God has laid before us and increase our commitment to see the gospel preached to all nations. The following passages are just a few verses that should stir up our urgency to take the gospel to all nations: Psalm 9:17, Ephesians 2:12, Romans 2:12, John 4:34-36, John 9:4, Luke 10:27, and Romans 10:13-14.

2. Make the Need Easy to Understand— As mobilizers, we talk about the unreached a lot. Our ultimate goal is to make the needs of the unreached more understandable and show Christians that the unreached are people just like you and me. They have some of the same dreams, fears, wants, and desires that you and I have. They are fathers, mothers, brothers, and sisters.

Make the unreached real to those you are mobilizing by introducing them to individual people groups. Show them photos of unreached people. Learn about their culture and religions. Invest in a world map and point out where these groups live. Discover if there are communities of unreached peoples in your city, state, or country to whom you can show Christ's love.

Use current events as a springboard to learn more about specific unreached peoples. For example, when this study was being written, the Philippines was recently devastated by Typhoon Haiyan. The Philippine Islands are home to dozens of unreached people groups. Mobilizers can use these events to fuel interest in and prayer for the unreached, and possibly even connect

believers to Christian aid groups and ministries working in affected areas.

When used correctly and in moderation, numbers or statistics can also help the church put the current state of world evangelization into perspective. It's helpful to put numbers in a context that is easy for people to relate to. For example, instead of saying there are 1.5 billion Muslims in 3,726 people groups, a mobilizer could say there are only six Christian workers for every 1 million Muslims. Using numbers in this way still shows the vast need among Muslims, but in a context that is easier to understand.

3. Show the Mission as Achievable— You've helped believers develop a sense of urgency, based on the Bible, to see the gospel proclaimed among all peoples. They are beginning to understand the current state of the world, where the gospel has already spread, and where it still needs to go. Now how do you move them into action? Over time, any commitment to frontier mission will fade and be forgotten if we fail to connect believers to practical ways they can participate in the Great Commission.

The best way that a mobilizer can connect believers to the task of world mission is by teaching the five habits of a World Christian. We will talk more about these in Lesson 6, but these habits are praying, sending, welcoming, going, and mobilizing.

A great way to encourage others to live the World Christian lifestyle is by telling stories of how everyday believers practice the habits of a World Christian. Share the stories of college students who gather weekly around a world map and pray for the nations. Tell stories about Christians who choose to live a simpler life so that they might invest more of their finances in supporting frontier mission work. Talk about the church that asked God to raise up 100 people from the congregation to go to the unreached and saw God answer their prayer! There is no shortage of inspirational examples of people who have found ways to use their time, talents, and resources for the kingdom. And telling these stories can help us show others what the World Christian lifestyle can look like. However, the best way is to be the story! Model what it means to love the unreached with practical activities every week. Soon you will have your own amazing stories to tell!

We truly live in an exciting time of gospel renewal, in a world where God is at work and people are being saved. Let's mobilize with a message of victory and joy. Let a desire to be a part of something big drive all believers to faithful obedience to the Great Commission.

GO ▶ DISCUSS

What would happen if the global Christian church embarked on a strategy to reach every people group with the gospel—a strategy that had an urgency and intensity similar to the world's when it banded together to rescue the 33 trapped miners?

_____

_____

_____

_____

_____

What would it take to help the church feel an urgency to see the gospel preached among every nation, tribe, people, and language? What hinders this urgency?

_____

_____

_____

_____

_____

What could help the global church prioritize the fulfillment of our call to reach all nations?

_____

_____

_____

_____

Mission mobilizers and leaders throughout history have adopted catch phrases or short sayings to help them rally others to mission. These short quotes were memorable, direct, and often convicting. Read aloud the quotes below. Which one impacts you the most?

- "And thus I aspire to preach the gospel, not where Christ was already named so that I would not build on another man's foundation." —**Paul (Rom 15:20)**

- "Christ for the students of the world, and the students of the world for Christ." —**Luther Wishard**

- "Here am I. Send me." —**Isaiah (Isa 6:8)**

- "We must be global Christians with a global vision because our God is a global God." —**John Stott**

- "If Jesus Christ be God and died for me, then no sacrifice can be too great for me to make for Him." —**C.T. Studd**

- "We have all eternity to celebrate our victories, but only one short hour before the sunset in which to win them." —**John Moffett**

- In response to the question of whether the heathen who have not heard the gospel will be saved: "It is more a question with me whether we, who have the gospel and fail to give it to those who have not, can be saved." —**C.H. Spurgeon**

- "The gospel is only good news if it arrives in time." —**Carl F.H. Henry**

- "We talk of the second coming; half the world has never heard of the first." —**Oswald J. Smith**

- "It is too small a thing for you to be my servant to restore the tribes of Jacob and bring back those of Israel I have kept. I will also make you a light for the Gentiles, that my salvation may reach to the ends of the earth." —**God (Isa 49:6)**

- "God has shown us more and more that there is no authentic Christianity that doesn't have a sense of urgency about evangelism." —**Pastor John Piper**

GO ▶ TO THE WORD

If there is an urgency in mission, then there will be an urgency in mobilization.
Read John 4:34-36 and Luke 10:2-3.

According to John 4, what were some of the driving forces behind Jesus' urgency that the gospel be preached?

_____
_____
_____
_____
_____
_____

In Luke 10:2, Jesus tells us "The harvest is plentiful, but the laborers are few. Therefore pray earnestly to the Lord of the harvest to send out laborers into his harvest." Then in verse 3, Jesus sends out His disciples to the harvest field. Why do you think Jesus started by telling His disciples to pray? What does prayer have to do with creating a sense of urgency in mission?

_____
_____
_____
_____
_____
_____

GO ▶ MOBILIZE

Pick an unreached people group, learn about them, and share your findings with three or more people. You can use www.joshuaproject.net to gather information, stories, and maybe even a picture. Consider finding and unreached people group being affected by a current world event in order to add more interest. Communicate these people's great need for Jesus, as well as the hope Jesus brings. See if they would pray with you right then! Perhaps they would be willing to join you in praying regularly for these people?

Pick a quote from the Go Discuss section that you found inspiring or convicting and put it somewhere you can read it daily. It could be next to your bed or desk, the background on your phone, or on your bathroom mirror. Consider changing the quote every week to keep a fresh sense of the urgency to reach the unreached.

GO ▶ PRAY

Urgency helps motivate the church to action. Spend time in prayer asking God to instill in your own hearts a sense of the acute need for all nations to be reached with the gospel. Ask Him to help you instill in others a sense of urgency that leads them to active involvement in frontier ministries.

THE 10/40 WINDOW:

67% OF THE WORLD'S POPULATION

82% OF THE WORLD'S POOR

97% OF THE WORLD'S UNREACHED PEOPLE

LESSON 4
MOBILIZING FROM SCRIPTURE: GOD'S WORD

"THEN [JESUS] OPENED THEIR MINDS SO THEY COULD UNDERSTAND THE SCRIPTURES. HE TOLD THEM, 'THIS IS WHAT IS WRITTEN [IN THE OLD TESTAMENT]: THE MESSIAH WILL SUFFER AND RISE FROM THE DEAD ON THE THIRD DAY, AND REPENTANCE FOR THE FORGIVENESS OF SINS WILL BE PREACHED IN HIS NAME TO ALL NATIONS, BEGINNING AT JERUSALEM.'" —LUKE 24:45-47

Several years back, I was sitting in a coffee shop reading the Word. When I opened my Bible, I found a bookmark a friend had given me years earlier. Printed on the bookmark was the "Biblical Basis of Missions," followed by a long list of Bible passages. I decided to take my friend's advice and read through all the verses in one sitting. I opened my Bible to the first passage, Genesis 12:1-3, and began to read. Half an hour later, after reading Revelation 7:9, I closed my Bible and sat quietly for a few minutes, in awe of God and His love for the nations.

At this point in my life, I had been mobilizing others for several years. I understood the biblical basis of missions and had taught it to others on a number of occasions. But when I sat down and read all these verses at once, I was overwhelmed by the unity of God's purpose. It excited me and made me want to share it with others.

God's desire to receive worship from all tribes, tongues, and nations is not just a theme of the Bible—it is the theme. Woven throughout the 66 books of the Bible is the redemptive message that God desires to fill the earth with His glory. And since the beginning, God's plan has included us.

The biblical basis of missions is the foundation from which we mobilize the body of Christ.

Whether one is preaching before many, teaching a few, discipling a select group, or even sharing over coffee, a mobilizer needs to be able to walk Christians through the Bible and show them that from Genesis to Revelation, God is on mission. We want to show that God's mission not only permeates the Bible, but is the glue that unites the stories of all 66 books.

As mobilizers, we must demonstrate beyond any doubt that our passion, motivation, and goal is thoroughly rooted in God's Word. Scripture teaches us, guides us, and is the final authority on all things, including mobilization. It must always be our most important resource to inform and invite Christians to join God on His mission. Therefore, we must be skilled in opening the Scriptures with Christians so they can see and hear God's passion and mission to reach all nations. For some Christians it will mean reading new verses and Bible stories they have never read before to see God's heart for all peoples. But for many, it will simply mean reading familiar stories and recognizing the global implication. We do not impose our ideas onto Scripture, but as we keep our eyes open to God's mission, the stories and verses become evident.

God loves to speak through His Word. Perhaps too often we don't give Him enough of an opportunity to do that. Certainly there is a place for information and statistics, but we must let the Word of God inform us, speak to us, and compel us to action.

So what are the fundamental and central biblical ideas a mobilizer needs to grasp in order to effectively teach the biblical basis of missions? Below are four key themes:

1. The Nature of Mission—Mission originated in the heart of God. It is not something we decide to do for God, but God reveals His purpose to us so that we may have a creative part in His mission. Make no mistake—we do not initiate the mission, nor will we consummate it.

2. The Global Thread—Mission is more than a collection of proof texts and isolated verses, but rather the driving narrative of Scripture. From Genesis to Revelation, God has been revealing through His Word His desire to reach all nations, tribes, peoples and languages. We call this continuity the global thread. An example can be found at the end of this lesson, and more resources are listed on page 42.

3. The Glory of God—Filling the earth with the glory of God is the reason mission exists. Planting churches and leading others to Christ is how we bring the glory of God to the nations. Mission is not about saving souls, but rather, it's about the worship these new believers bring to our Lord. The more we study God's Word with His glory in mind, the more we will see that missions is not about us or what we do. We must always remember that God and His glory are the ultimate goal. "All the nations you have made shall come and worship before you, O Lord, and shall glorify your name" (Psalm 86:9).

4. The Role of the Believer—While mission is about the glory of God and not the work of man, God has appointed man to be His chosen instrument. Therefore, teaching the biblical basis shows believers just how important they are in the fulfillment of God's plan.

We want to instill in the people we mobilize a conviction to take personal responsibility for helping complete the Great Commission. Essentially, we want them to ask themselves, in light of this conviction, "Is the vision I have for my life big enough?"

God's vision for His Son Jesus Christ is recorded in Isaiah 49:6. "He says: 'It is too small a thing for you to be my servant to restore the tribes of Jacob and bring back those of Israel I have kept. I will also make you a light for the Gentiles, that my salvation may reach to the ends of the earth.'"

If a believer's vision for their life, family, and ministry does not include the nations, then it is not big enough. If they believe that mission is regulated to those who have been specifically called, then it is not big enough. Pastor John Piper says it best when he says, "The way a believer sees their role in relation to world mission will depend on their vision of God and their view of man. And these in turn depend primarily upon their grasp of Scripture and secondarily upon their awareness of our contemporary global situation."

In this lesson, we focused on the biblical basis. In the next lesson, we will help you become more aware of the world and why we believe mobilizers should emphasize the least reached, unreached, and unengaged.

GO ▶ DISCUSS

What verses and stories are most significant to you regarding God's global mission? Which have you seen are most impactful to others?

With so much of the biblical narrative calling both the local church and individual believers to join God in His global mission, why is it that so few see it as a central theme?

_____

_____

_____

Read Psalm 46:10. Many Christians around the world can recite the first half of this verse by heart, but don't know the second half. Can you think of other familiar verses or stories where the theme of mission is present, but overlooked?

_____

_____

_____

What do you think are the important aspects of sharing the biblical basis of missions?

_____

_____

_____

GO ▶ TO THE WORD

Read Psalm 67 together as a group.

How many of you are familiar with Psalm 67:1? How many of you are familiar with verse 2? How is Psalm 67:1-2 similar to Psalm 46:10?

_____

_____

_____

Count the number of times the words *nations, earth,* or *peoples* appear in Psalm 67. Why do you feel the Psalmist chose to repeat these words?

_____

_____

_____

GO ▶ MOBILIZE

Begin memorizing Genesis 12:1-3; Psalm 46:10; Isaiah 49:6; Matthew 28:19-20; and Revelation 7:9. Try to have all five verses memorized before Lesson 7. Commit to holding each other accountable each week for memorizing these passages. You will use these verses in Lesson 7 to draw out a comprehensive diagram, "The Window to the Nations," that explains the three steps to mobilization you are learning about in this study. This illustration will be a simple and effective way to begin a conversation that challenges your friends to think globally.

Take 30 to 40 minutes this week to read the verses on the next page that offer a small glimpse of the global thread throughout Scripture. Do this in one uninterrupted sitting. Reflect on the theme of these passages and allow yourself to have a fresh encounter with God and his global passion. Then, ask one to three people to do the same thing with you.

Gen 1:28	Deut 4:5-6	Isa 49:6	Rom 1:5
Gen 9:1	Josh 2:9-11	Mal 1:11	Rom 15:20
Gen 11:1-9	1 Sam 17:45-56	Matt 24:14	Rev 5:9
Gen 12:1-5	1 Kings 10:23-24	Matt 28:18-20	Rev 7:9-10
Gen 26:3-4	Ps 67:1-7	Luke 4:42-43	
Gen 28:13-15	Dan 3:28-29	Acts 1:8	

GO ▶ PRAY

Spend time praying that God would speak to you through His Word, showing you the vast extent of His global vision.

Pray that your vision for your life, your family, and your church will be as big as God's vision. Pray that God will prepare you, your family, and your church to discover and play their most strategic role in God's mission to reach all peoples.

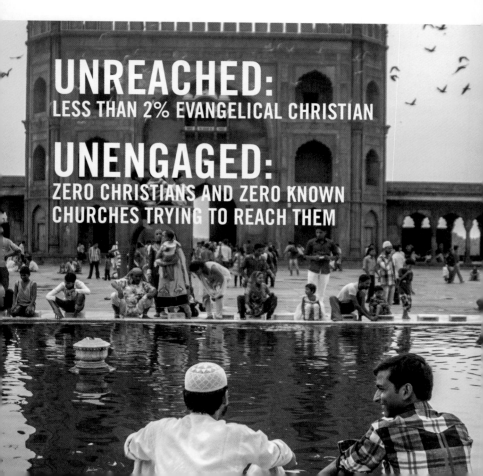

UNREACHED:
LESS THAN 2% EVANGELICAL CHRISTIAN

UNENGAGED:
ZERO CHRISTIANS AND ZERO KNOWN
CHURCHES TRYING TO REACH THEM

LESSON 5
MOBILIZING TO THE UNREACHED: GOD'S WORLD

"I NOW REALIZE THAT GOD IS ALREADY OUT THERE WORKING AMONG THE UNREACHED; AND HE IS CALLING FOR ME TO COME JOIN HIM." —A YOUNG NIGERIAN BELIEVER

Now is the time for mobilizers worldwide to sound the call for the body of Christ to prioritize mission to the unreached! Today, we need discerning followers of God, just like the "men from Issachar" in 1 Chronicles 12:32. They understood the times, they understood what God wanted to do in Israel, and they mobilized their whole families and tribe to accomplish that goal.

What would it take for us to mobilize the global church toward the goal of completing the Great Commission? In the next lesson, we will learn practical steps for how to mobilize others to their strategic role in God's global purpose. But first, we need to understand our own times and the current state of God's world so we know what God wants us to do.

As Christians, we are adopted sons and daughters in God's family. We have the blessing of being reconciled to God through Christ, the opportunity to come before God daily for renewal, and the power of Holy Spirit living within us. But put yourself in the shoes of someone today who is living with no access to Jesus.

You are living in the 10/40 window, but you have no idea what that is. You have never heard the name of Jesus, so the idea that you are unreached has never crossed your mind. There is no church you can attend on Sunday morning to hear the gospel. There are no bookstores where you can purchase a Bible. There are no Christians whom you can go to and ask about their hope in Christ, and there is no mission effort focused on reaching you.

You are living in a sea of people, as one among millions. No one is trying to share the life-giving truth of salvation with you. You are utterly unengaged with the gospel. You have no access.

OUR RESPONSIBILITY AS GOD'S CHURCH

It is the calling of each believer to play his or her strategic role in taking the hope of the gospel to those who have no hope. Paul, who focused on taking the gospel to the unreached of his day, described us as "Christ's ambassadors, as though God were making his appeal through us" (2 Cor 5:20). God has chosen to reach His world through us, His church.

As mobilizers, we celebrate everyone who labors with Christ on behalf of His church. We also recognize the imbalance between those laboring among peoples who already have access to the gospel and those who do not have access.

We rejoice that on average, those in the reached part of the world are exposed to the gospel, in one form or another, more than once a day. At the same time, however, a vast majority of the 2.91 billion people who are unreached do not know anyone who knows anyone who knows Jesus. The issue is not that a local church is passive in reaching out to them, but rather that there are no local churches to reach out to them. They live their whole lives never meeting any followers of Christ, never seeing their joy, never feeling their love, and never being prayed for.

It's not a matter of who is worthy to hear the gospel because God desires all to come to repentance (2 Peter 3:9). Rather, it is a matter of access to the gospel. It is not that my lost neighbor is any more or less lost, or more or less valuable to God than the person living in a city in northern India. However, my unsaved neighbor is surrounded by people who could share Christ with him. My unsaved neighbor likely drives past dozens of churches on his way to work or school. But the man or woman in northern India passes no churches on the way to work, nor has any friends or neighbors who could share the gospel. They have no access.

MAJOR WORLD RELIGIONS

To help us remember and teach others, we have organized the lost throughout the world into five mega-groups, which can be remembered using the English acronym THUMB. It provides us with a snapshot of the church's current effort in sending Christians workers to reach the world with the blessing of hope and salvation through Jesus.

Jesus' statement in Acts 1:8 does not say "first reach Jerusalem, and then after that reach Judea and Samaria, and then after that reach the ends of the earth." The grammatical structure clearly shows it is a both/and statement. Biblically, we have a responsibility and an empowerment for all three. We don't all go, but we all get to play a part in reaching those at the ends of the earth who have no access!

Just as the Holy Spirit empowered the early church, the body of Christ can be empowered today to bring the message of salvation to all peoples in our lifetime. Jesus' first disciples understood God's world and most of them spent their lives preaching the gospel where it wasn't known. They preached and were martyred anywhere from 1200 to 3100 km away from Jerusalem (that's a long way to walk). They traveled as far as southern Ethiopia, most of northern Africa, throughout the Roman Empire, up to the British Isles, across Arabia, into Persia and even India! They did this by focusing their attention, resources and manpower on being a blessing to all peoples.

Many others have followed in their footsteps throughout history and now have passed the baton on to our generation of Christ-followers. How will we rise to the occasion to complete this remaining task in our lifetime?

Today, evangelical Christianity is the fastest growing religious group, with 546 million adherents worldwide. As the body of Christ, we have the people, the resources in our hands, and most importantly, the Holy Spirit empowering our lives as we labor to complete Jesus' commission to us!

We can reach the unreached. We can engage the unengaged. But the task calls for every follower of Jesus in the global church to be mobilized to his or her strategic role in fulfilling God's Great Commission.

Tribal
60 cross-cultural workers for every 1 million people
Hindu
2 cross-cultural workers for every 1 million people
Unreligious
12 cross-cultural workers for every 1 million people
Muslim
6 cross-cultural workers for every 1 million people
Buddhist
13 cross-cultural workers for every 1 million people

GO ▶ DISCUSS

After looking at the highlighted box in the text, do those numbers surprise you?

How do you feel when you think about people around the world who are just like you, your family, and your friends except they have no viable access to Jesus?

_____

_____

_____

_____

Information rarely brings transformation in someone's life, however the right information coupled with revelation from God does transform. How can we use Scripture and the state of the world to mobilize Christians from belief to conviction?

_____

_____

_____

_____

How would you respond to someone saying "Yes, but we need missionaries in our own city or country too?"

_____

_____

_____

_____

GO ▶ TO THE WORD

Read Romans 10:9-15 and 15:18-24.

Right after Paul's famous words in 10:9-10 about salvation, what does he immediately focus on in verses 13-15? Who does he want to reach? Who does he want to be involved?

_____

_____

_____

_____

In Romans 15, Paul cites Old Testament verses conveying that God has always desired Gentiles (all ethnic groups outside of Israel) to be saved. Based on 15:18-24, discuss who Paul wanted to minister to, where he wanted to go, and who he wanted to send him. In light of verse 20, what did Paul mean in the first half of verse 23? What insights do we gain from this about Paul's attitude toward missions?

_____

_____

_____

_____

GO ▶ MOBILIZE

Memorize the THUMB acronym and how many cross-cultural workers there are per million people for each religious group.

Identify three people you want to share the THUMB acronym with. Use this information to start a conversation about the status of the world from God's perspective. Let them feel the weight of how few laborers there are, but also inspire them that in God's eyes the harvest is plentiful. See if they will pray with you right then for more laborers.

GO ▶ PRAY

Pray that God would give you His heart, passion, and desire for those who have never heard of Jesus to be introduced to the hope and salvation found through Him.

As your heart is being transformed into God's heart, pray that the Holy Spirit would use you to spark this same transformation in others.

The need is large and urgent. Pray for the lost throughout the world to hear of Jesus and for the church to mobilize its time and resources in accordance with God's heart and the great need.

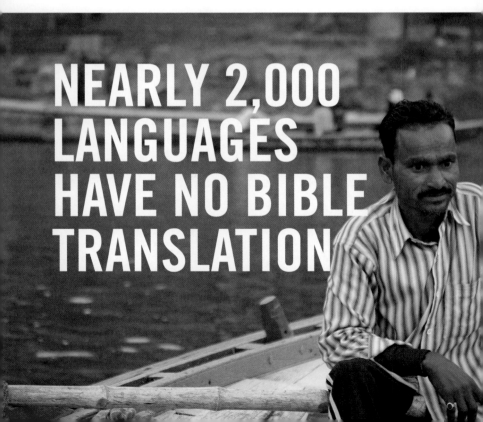

NEARLY 2,000 LANGUAGES HAVE NO BIBLE TRANSLATION

LESSON 6
MOBILIZING TO STRATEGIC PRACTICES: GOD'S WORK

"THERE IS A YOU-SHAPED VOID IN THE GREAT COMMISSION. FIND IT AND FILL IT!" —PATRICK JOHNSTONE

God extends an invitation and places a calling on each Christian's life to be a part of His global story in reaching all peoples of the earth with the gospel. Some Christians best play out their part in this story by laboring on the mission field, but that is only one among many roles God has designed for His people to play.

Recall back to Lesson 1, when we compared mission mobilization to preparing troops for war. While one soldier is working hard on the front lines of battle, there are many more people working behind the scenes to support him in his work. The soldiers cannot be successful in their mission without people filling these behind-the-scenes roles in administration, technology, communication, human resources, and more.

The same is true for mission. God has created each of us with talents, skills, gifts, and abilities that can be harnessed to fulfill specific roles in reaching all peoples with the gospel—whether that means working in frontier mission or serving in strategic roles on the home front. World Christians are believers who have realized they have a part to play in the expansion of God's Kingdom on earth. They have committed to prioritizing their lives around their desire to see God glorified by every people group on earth. They channel their time, money, careers, decisions, dreams, and more into the specific role God has created for

them to play within His global story.

THE BASIS OF WORLD CHRISTIAN CULTURE
The crucial foundation to creating a culture of World Christians is the understanding of what mission is. We believe there is no greater labor than working to see God receive glory from all peoples. The Bible reads as one large narrative, telling the story of how God is on a mission to redeem all humanity to Himself. Jesus accomplished the work of redemption and then chose to work through His people, the church, to preach this redemption to all nations. His intent in redeeming us was not only so we could have a personal relationship with Him, but also so we could join Him on His mission. In this way, through our lives and the lives of countless others, God gets the glory He deserves. When we understand this foundation, it helps us realize the great worth of the cause and align our existence around it. When we realize that we all have a part to play in God's plan, we can then turn our hearts toward God's purposes and begin to devote our talents, interests, and careers toward His glory.

WORLD CHRISTIAN LIFESTYLE
So what does this look like practically? We have identified five ways that World Christians are involved in the Great Commission. These five practices are the natural result of any Christian aligning his or her existence with the purpose of seeing God glorified among the nations.

1. Praying for the Nations—The most foundational of the five habits of a World Christian is prayer. God has invited us to be a part of His work across the globe, and without His power, our work will come to nothing. Every World Christian should find themselves praying for the unreached in different nations, cross-cultural workers laboring in those nations, and the advancement of God's kingdom around the world. The need for Jesus to bring salvation and end violence, oppression, exploitation, and tyranny around the world calls for deep prayer. Praying for the nations will change your life and change the world. See a list of mission-based prayer resources on page 42.

2. Going to the Nations—God desires to use His church in advancing His Kingdom and establishing the presence of the gospel in places where His truth is not yet known. Going is responding to God's open invitation to step into cross-cultural ministry as a church planter, business entrepreneur, social justice worker, and more. God has chosen His children to be ambassadors of His gospel, and ambassadors must go. Going can mean selling everything you own and moving your whole family to another country. Or it can mean going for a shorter period of time. Whether you go for a week, a year, or for a lifetime, the point is to go!

3. Sending Workers to the Nations—To send is to leverage one's career, money, skills, and influence to send and support people engaged in cross-cultural ministry. Sending is supporting through prayer, finances, logistics, encouragement, and more. Senders are the support network of every cross-cultural worker—a group of people who are prepared to uphold them in times of celebration, as well as in times of need. Sending is a crucial role in leveraging one's life to sustain the work of the goer (Rom 10:15).

4. Welcoming the Nations—In today's ever-shrinking world, one habit of the World Christian often overlooked is welcoming the internationals that live in your home country. When we cannot go to the nations, often God brings them to us. Whether you live in a big city or a small town, it is likely that you are living close to an international student, a migrant worker, or maybe even refugees. By inviting internationals into your life, you will have a chance to share the gospel with someone who may never have had access to it before meeting you. Without ever leaving your home country, you can play a part in God's plan to redeem people from every people group on earth.

5. Mobilizing Others to the Nations—The harvest is plentiful, but the laborers are few. Unfortunately, many Christians live most of their years in the church never realizing that they have a part to play in something much bigger than themselves. The work of the mobilizer is to point these people who know Jesus to their vital role in reaching those who don't know Jesus.

Mobilization is something all of us can make a part of our lifestyles. In some sense, we are already mobilizers; that is, whatever we love, we inevitably try to get others to love as well. Whether it is a movie, a toy, a tool, or a vacation spot, we tell people about the things we enjoy and want them to be just as excited as we are. God does that too. He is passionate about reaching those who have never heard the gospel, and He loves when we get excited about it too! Mobilizing people to the unreached is simply sharing God's excitement, and ours, in such a way that people can't help but catch our passion for His glory and want to be involved in spreading it to all over the world. In this way, we can all mobilize. Whether you mobilize one person a year, one hundred, or one thousand, all of us can easily make the ministry of mobilization part of our lifestyle.

THE PRACTICAL DIFFERENCE

The goal of mobilization is to change believers' convictions so that in every season of life, their priorities and lifestyle will reflect God's heart for all nations. Some will actively be doing all five practices at the same time, but most likely there will be seasons in life where people participate in two or three of these practices far more than the others. However, we have missed the mark if people choose one practice just so they can check off their "missions" box and then cease to participate in God's global mission. That is why we emphasize the World Christian lifestyle instead of just getting people to sign a pledge to go live in another country. God has appointed a complex task to His people and there are many roles to fill. By establishing a World Christian culture among our churches, we will see countless believers raised up to find their most strategic role, and working as a team, they will pull together to advance the kingdom of God across the world in a sustainable and powerful way. It is a paradigm shift that will make a lasting impact on the lives of the Christians in the church today.

Mobilization is all about modeling these World Christian practices and inviting others into our lives to do them with us. Our example, more than our words, will compel and empower others to join in this lifestyle. By walking with people through this journey, we can help them set achievable goals so they stay interested, grow in excitement, and start changing their weekly routine to reflect God's heart for the world.

Through our words and actions, we can inspire our fellow believers to recognize the great and high purpose of seeking God's glory among the nations. When we have succeeded in helping Christians see their lives as roles in God's global story, we will have established a World Christian culture that will affect them for a lifetime. Then we can watch as this change spreads throughout the church, establishing a movement of Christians who are aligning their lives with God's story of redemption across the world.

GO ▶ DISCUSS

As you discuss each of the five habits of a World Christian, brainstorm creative ways that you can begin practicing or continue each of them.

PRAYER FOR THE NATIONS

What are ways you can pray more regularly, more informed, and more passionately for the unreached? In what ways can you ask others to join you? Idea: Consider finding a picture of someone from an unreached people group and making it the background on your phone or computer. Use it as a prompt to say a prayer for that people group every time you see the picture.

_____

_____

_____

_____

_____

GOING TO THE NATIONS

What are the stereotypical descriptions of a "missionary" in your church, your generation, and your culture? What is true and what is not true of those descriptions?

_____

_____

_____

_____

Are there beneficial and strategic ways you or others you know could participate in going? Idea: Consider taking a weekend trip to an area with unreached people. Try to meet some of the people there to learn about them and their culture. Who would you take with you?

_____

_____

_____

_____

_____

SENDING WORKERS TO THE NATIONS

Sending is a multifaceted role. In what creative ways could you regularly support, encourage, and participate in the lives of goers? Idea: Consider writing a letter of encouragement to the same missionary once a month. Who could you challenge to join you in financially supporting a goer?

_____

_____

_____

_____

_____

WELCOMING THE NATIONS

What groups of internationals are in your area? Where is the nearest Muslim mosque, Buddhist temple, or Hindu temple?

_____

_____

_____

_____

_____

How might you, your friends, and your church engage internationals and minister to their needs? Idea: When you go out to eat, go to an ethnic restaurant and build a relationship with the owners.

_____

_____

_____

_____

_____

MOBILIZING OTHERS

What are some of the most effective ways that you have found to get people excited about God's heart for all nations? Idea: Plan an ethnic evening to cook a meal from another culture. Invite a few of your friends and learn together about an unreached people group from that culture.

_____

_____

_____

_____

_____

GO ▶ TO THE WORD

Read 1 Corinthians 12:12-26 and discuss the following questions:

Just like all the parts of the body must be present and working together, discuss how all the aspects of the World Christian lifestyle are necessary. What happens if one or more of the aspects is missing?

_____
_____
_____
_____

Invariably, whenever someone teaches on mission, some people listening will think the message does not apply to them because they "have not been called to mission." How can we use this passage to help a person understand the importance of his or her part in the fulfillment of the Great Commission?

_____
_____
_____
_____
_____

GO ▶ MOBILIZE

Before we can mobilize others to the World Christian lifestyle, we need to evaluate our own lifestyle. Which of these roles do you do well? Which ones are harder for you? It is good to work on the areas you are weak in so you can be well rounded, but feel free to spend most of your time inviting people into the areas you are strong in and passionate about.

_____
_____
_____

Invite three people to join you in at least one activity as you live out an aspect of the World Christian Lifestyle. Make sure you prepare well whether you are praying together, writing an encouraging letter to missionaries, or welcoming.

_____
_____
_____
_____
_____

GO ▶ PRAY

Pray and ask God that your life would glorify Him above all. Pray that your own walk with the Lord would model the World Christian lifestyle to those around you.

IF 0.1% OF AFRICAN EVANGELICALS WERE MOBILIZED TO GO,

IT WOULD BE THE LARGEST MISSION MOVEMENT IN HISTORY

LESSON 7
GO MOBILIZE!
HOW TO BEGIN

"MOBILIZE ME AND I'LL CHANGE MY WORLD!"
—CAMPAIGN SLOGAN FOR WORLD BICYCLE RELIEF

SPARK A MISSION MOVEMENT WHERE YOU LIVE

You can make a difference where you live! As a mobilizer, your sights should be set on nothing less than sparking a mission movement in your area. This is the vision. Who wouldn't want to be a part of a movement that resulted in believers of every type, personality, and skill set connecting to their most strategic role in fulfilling the Great Commission? It might sound overwhelming, but there are two simple things you can do today that will launch you on your way toward sparking a mission movement where you live. Don't get me wrong—the work of a mobilizer can appear multi-faceted and complex. But focusing on these two principles will bring simplicity and clarity to your vision and next steps. The work of the mobilizer is not a burden. It is a joy when you have the right perspective and the right priorities.

JOIN GOD AT WORK

The first principle in sparking a mission movement where you live is to concentrate your efforts where God is already at work. Somewhere in your church, city, or on your university campus, there are Christians like you who want to make a difference with their lives. These believers may already be thinking about going to the nations. They may already be praying for the nations. Somewhere near you, no doubt, there may be a few like-minded people who are ready to team up with you to spark a mission movement.

The solo mobilizer quickly loses steam and burns out. But when we find where God is already at work in the hearts of other local believers and join forces with them, we gain momentum and become more effective. This may be a small group Bible study focused on God's heart for the nations. It could be a Perspectives or a Kairos class. It may be a church where several members are taking mission trips, learning more about cross-cultural ministry, and dreaming about making a greater impact around the world. It may be on your campus among fellow students who love and serve Jesus. Start where there is a passion for Jesus and work from there. In other words, pour gasoline on the places where the embers are already glowing. Go where there is existing momentum and connect with one, two, or three believers. Share your vision for sparking a mission movement. Take inventory of what assets and resources your small group or church has that may help accelerate greater mission awareness. Then put a plan together.

Don't do it alone. Find partners, mentors, and friends who care about the same things you care about. Get with them, pray with them and begin to plan. If they are far away, then use Skype, email or phone calls. Set regular meeting times or calls when your group can discuss a mobilization plan for a particular target audience.

MULTIPLYING MOBILIZERS

The second principle is to build a network of leaders you will develop as mobilizers. Think about the logic of this for a moment. If our goal is to send out more and more laborers into the harvest, then we will need people dedicating themselves to the ministry of mobilizing the laborers to action (see *YOU HAVE GREAT POTENTIAL AS A MOBILIZER* in the appendix, page 41). But the natural question is this: if the mobilizer is developing those who go, send, pray, and welcome, who is developing the mobilizers?

This brings us to the next tier of building a mission movement. We need mobilizers who will apportion some amount of their ministry time to the task of developing other emerging mobilizers. This is the key to a long-term, sustainable mission movement.

Think for a moment about what would happen if this were not the case. If mobilizers focused only on developing people to go, welcome, pray, and send, they would not duplicate themselves. All of the work would rest upon that small group of mobilizers. Instead, when mobilizers develop other mobilizers, they multiply themselves several fold, and the movement is able to expand exponentially.

Let me illustrate how focusing time on developing mobilizers speeds up the work tremendously. Could you guess what the outcome would be if every year you helped four people become World Christians, one person become a goer, and one person become a mobilizer — and then every year both you and the new mobilizer(s) repeated that same process? After 20 years there would be 4 million World Christians, 1 million mobilizers, and 1 million goers among the unreached! Can you imagine the impact for Christ among the nations? This is when a ministry becomes a movement. This is the power of multiplication. And the result is a longer, healthier, more sustainable mission movement.

FIVE STEPS

As you apply these two guiding principles, there are five important developmental steps you will take.

1. Pray—As a mobilizer, your first step is to align your heart with God's purpose. Just like Nehemiah, your first step in forming a strategy should start by spending extended time with the Lord. Synchronize your heart and passion to His Word and His purpose. Ask God to direct you as you meet other leaders and form a team.

2. Identify—Find out where God is already at work around you. Who are those people you can align with to pray and plan a mobilization strategy? Are there existing strategies already in play within your community that you could join? Or do you need to start a new strategy and build it from the ground up? Find others who have a passion for cross-cultural ministry. Build relationships. Build your network.

3. Resource—This is where your plan comes into play. Determine what your strategy will be. How will you help believers become World Christians? How will you resource them to go, mobilize, welcome, pray, and send? How often will you meet with your growing network of leaders? Which resources are most pertinent to your target audience? Get buy-in from a few key people. Don't carry the strategy alone. Finally, identify the win. In other words, how will you and your team know you are making progress? What are your success criteria?

4. Execute—Don't be afraid to fail here. You will undoubtedly have missteps. Don't let that deter you. Everyone falls down. But the distinguishing characteristic of a good leader is the determination to get up and press onward. Be confident that you are aligned with God's heart and purpose. He is with you!

5. Develop Others—This is key. As you and your team execute your strategy, you must be developing leaders as you go. Develop other mobilizers. Invite them along with you to see how you are mobilizing your target audience. Challenge them to do the same. Take them through *Go Mobilize*. Release them to mobilize in a target audience and provide feedback. Finally, send them out. You'll be amazed at how God will use you to raise up other mobilizers.

In summary, go where God is at work and join Him there. Stoke the embers of mission enthusiasm and excitement where you live.

Search for and connect with other like-minded Christians to build a team, and identify your target audience for mobilization—a church, a network of churches, a college campus, or a ministry. Then build a leadership network of mobilizers who can help you execute a plan for mobilization. Get familiar with mobilization tools and resources like Perspectives, Kairos, NVision, *Xplore*, and other tools. Figure out which tools or combination of resources best fit into your plan. Pray like crazy, and see how great your impact will be on the nations!

GO ▶ DISCUSS

Where in your church or community is God already moving people toward engaging the nations?

What would it look like for you to join God in what He is already doing among the Christians in your community who are working to engage the nations? How could you gather some of these men and/or women together to build a mobilization team?

In general, who is the most natural target audience for you? Are there specific groups within that target audience who would be more effective to start with?

Which resources do you think are best to use in mobilizing this particular target audience? Consider time constraints, level of education, culture, and other factors as you choose.

GO ▶ TO THE WORD

Read Nehemiah 1.

Describe Nehemiah's reaction after he received the news about the state of his homeland.

_____
_____
_____
_____
_____
_____

What process did Nehemiah go through before he was able to place a single brick in the wall in Jerusalem? Describe the steps he took.

_____
_____
_____
_____
_____
_____

How might Nehemiah's situation parallel the task of a mobilizer who seeks to stir his people toward engaging God's global purposes?

_____
_____
_____
_____
_____
_____

GO ▶ MOBILIZE

Start working on a mobilization plan: write down your dreams, outline your mobilization ideas, and list some practical next steps. Spend some more time as a group or as individuals thinking about the strategy questions from this chapter.

GO ▶ PRAY

Take some time now to pray about your next step as a mobilizer. Ask God to help you form a team. Ask God to do great things among the nations in your church, ministry, or school. Remember the words of William Carey, who said, "Attempt great things for God. Expect great things from God." Have this same faith. God is with you every step of the way. _Go mobilize._

TAKE THE PLEDGE

Empowered and guided by the Holy Spirit, I commit to living my life in light of God's Word, God's world, and God's work.

I embrace the biblical basis of missions and will continue to review and study it in God's Word.

I will continue learning about the unreached, rejoicing in the church's successes and staying up to date on the task remaining in God's world.

I commit to living the World Christian lifestyle and mobilizing others to join in God's work.

AS GOD ALLOWS, I WILL MODEL THIS THROUGH:

- Praying regularly for the unreached
- Taking opportunities to go to the unreached as the Lord directs
- Participating in sending goers to the unreached
- Welcoming internationals around me
- Seeking opportunities around me to mobilize others to the unreached
- Identifying, encouraging, developing, and releasing other mobilizers

Signed _____ Date _____

APPENDIX

SHARE THE WINDOW

The Window is an excellent way to invite people into exploring a World Christian lifestyle. In a simple sketch you can help people look through The Window to see God's perspective on His Word, His world, the work He has called us to do, and what our role is in His global mission. The Window will help you share the Bible verses you have memorized, as well as the THUMB acronym. Check out how it works.

EXAMPLE OF THE WINDOW COMPLETED

1 GOD'S WORD	2 GOD'S WORLD
Gen 12:1-3; Ps 46:10; Isa 49:6; Matt 28:19-20; and Rev 7:9 **Survey of the Bible in 5**	Tribal, Hindu, Unreligious, Muslim & Buddhist **5 THUMB**
3 GOD'S WORK	4
Going, Sending, Welcoming, Mobilizing & Praying **5 Habits**	**?**

HOW TO BEGIN

TRANSITION 1: Start off by asking your friend if he or she has ever heard of the World Christian lifestyle or understands what it means to be a World Christian.

ACTION: Draw the Window with the four panes in the middle. Leave the diagram blank for now.

EXPLANATION: Explain that by using this window diagram, we can see more clearly God's perspective on His Word, His world, the work He has called us to do, and how we can fit into His global mission.

GOD'S WORD	GOD'S WORLD
GOD'S WORK	

TRANSITION 2: Say, "But in order for us to understand God's global purposes and to join with Him in the most strategic way possible, there are three areas we need to understand. These three are: ..."

ACTION: Label the top left box "God's Word," the top right box "God's World," and the bottom left box "God's Work." Leave the bottom right box blank for now.

EXPLANATION: Explain that World Christians are simply Christians who have a global perspective on their Christian life. They have come to understand these three areas: God's Word, God's world, and God's work, and they live their lives based on this.

1 GOD'S WORD
Gen 12:1-3; Ps 46:10; Isa 49:6; Matt 28:19-20; and Rev 7:9
Survey of the Bible in 5

TRANSITION 3: Starting with God's Word, ask your friend if he or she knows any verses that deal with mission or with the nations. Write any of these verses somewhere to the side of the Window.

ACTION: Now tell your friend that the Bible is full of verses about God's love for the nations, but we are going to focus on five. Write the phrase "Survey of the Bible in 5" in the box labeled God's Word. Then list out: Gen 12:1-3, Ps 46:10, Isa 49:6, Matt 28:19-20, Rev 7:9.

EXPLANATION: Spend a few minutes going over the five verses, pausing to explain how each verse shows God's global purpose. It's good to have a Bible with you as you share, but we also encourage you to have the verses memorized.

2 GOD'S WORLD
Tribal, Hindu, Unreligious, Muslim & Buddhist
5 THUMB

TRANSITION 4: "We just read that God desires to reach all nations and peoples with His gospel. In light of this, a World Christian needs know what the world looks like today and what people groups have not yet heard the gospel message. Currently, almost all unreached people are members of one of these five mega groups."

ACTION: Write the number "5," and next to it the THUMB acronym in the top right box labeled God's world. Say something like: "If you can remember your thumb, then you can remember 90 percent of the world's unreached people groups." You can also write the number "10" outside the bottom right corner of the diagram and the number "40" outside the top right corner. Use these two numbers to explain the 10/40 Window, the geographical area where most of the world's unreached live.

EXPLANATION: Explain the five mega groups: Tribal, Hindu, Unreligious, Muslim, and Buddhist. Explain to your friend that very little of the global church's attention is focused on these five groups—that they receive less than 10 percent of the church's missionary efforts and less than 0.1 percent of its financial resources. Mention the ratio of Christian workers per million unreached (see page 24). For example, there are only 2 workers per one million Hindus. In contrast, explain how the majority of the global church's time, talent, and treasure go to reach places that are already strongly Christian. Make sure you explain the difference between the reached and unreached.

3 GOD'S WORK
Going, Sending, Welcoming, Mobilizing & Praying
5 Habits

TRANSITION 5: "In light of God's Word and the needs in God's world, the World Christian is engaging in God's work. And they do this by practicing the '5 Habits of a World Christian.'"

ACTION: Write "5 Habits" in the box labeled God's Work. On the side, from top to bottom, list out the five habits: Praying, Sending, Welcoming, Going, and Mobilizing.

EXPLANATION: Go through each of the habits, explaining what they mean. Ask your friend why we call these "habits" and not "choices." Explain that we can and should be practicing multiple habits (maybe even all five), but not merely picking one or two just to check off our list of good Christian deeds. Share what you are doing to live out a World Christian lifestyle and point your friend to opportunities to adopt similar habits.

TRANSITION 6: "So far we have looked at God's Word and how he desires to reach all peoples. We've looked at God's world and have a better understanding of the task remaining. And we just looked at the 5 habits of World Christians. Now it's time we give an honest assessment of our own lives."

ACTION: In the last pane of the window draw a question mark.

INITIATION: Ask your friend, "Now that we have briefly looked into this window to see God's Word, God's world, and God's work, would you like to learn more?" If your friend says "yes," give a few minutes to talk about what interests him or her. Afterward, use those interests to extend an invitation to some next steps, most likely to go through the *Xplore* study with you. Explain how the *Xplore* study helps people grow in the area that interests him or her, plus all the others as well. Schedule a day and time to begin *Xplore* and then write it on the diagram. Let your friend keep the diagram.

CONCLUSION: Take a few minutes and pray together.

YOU HAVE GREAT POTENTIAL AS A MOBILIZER

After reading *Go Mobilize* we hope you are encouraged, equipped, and inspired to mobilize others to begin considering unreached people groups as a part of their faith walk with Jesus. You now have the knowledge and resources to help others discover God's Word, God's world, and God's work. Here's an example of what God can do though your faith if you were to begin leading one small group of six people per year through *Xplore*.

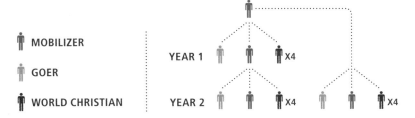

MOBILIZER

GOER

WORLD CHRISTIAN

YEAR 1

YEAR 2

The ultimate goal of mobilization is to see goers take the Gospel to the unreached, but we also must continue to raise up even more World Christians who aid in and support the missions movement and mobilizers who multiply it. So by God's grace, you might see one person in your small group study commit to being a goer, one partnering with you to mobilize others, and the other 4 faithfully living out the World Christian lifestyle.

If you, as a mobilizer, multiplied your life each year for 20 years through this small group setting, and a new mobilizer was raised up from each group, there would be 4 million World Christians, 1 million mobilizers, and 1 million goers among the unreached! Imagine the impact for Christ among the nations!

GO MOBILIZE!

RESOURCES

For more resources to help mobilize your family, friends, and church, go to mobilization.org/resources.

- *Xplore* (in multiple languages)
- *Go Mobilize* (in multiple languages)
- Coaching Conversations for mobilizers
- Resources for mobilizing children and families
- NVision Seminar
- Practical ideas for living out the 5 habits of the World Christian lifestyle
- Resources on the biblical basis of missions
- Personal support raising
- For the 7- or 30-Day Challenge on the biblical basis of mission, go to mobilization.org/challenges.

OTHER STATISTICS AND PRAYER RESOURCES
- thenations.us
- joshuaproject.org
- grd.imb.org
- thetravelingteam.org .
- aboutmissions.org
- operationworld.org

ACKNOWLEDGMENTS

Go Mobilize was created by Jason G (Lessons 1, 2, 3, 4), Mike K (Lessons 1, 7), Mike T (Lesson 6), Titus H (Lesson 5, editing), and Bethany S (editor). Together, this team of mission mobilizers has a combined 71 years in cross-cultural and domestic ministry. Primary places they have or are currently working are Russia, Ukraine, Brazil, the Middle East, East Asia, American university campuses, and with international students in the USA.